WRITING THAT CHANGED U.S. HISTORY

DECLARATION OF INDEPENDENCE

by Josephine Larsen

I0816573

pogo

Pogo Books, an imprint of Jump! Library by FlutterBee

Ideas for Parents and Teachers

Pogo Books let children practice reading informational text while introducing them to nonfiction features such as headings, labels, sidebars, maps, and diagrams, as well as a table of contents, glossary, and index.

Carefully leveled text with a strong photo match offers early fluent readers the support they need to succeed.

Before Reading

- "Walk" through the book and point out the various nonfiction features. Ask the student what purpose each feature serves.
- Look at the glossary together. Read and discuss the words.

During Reading

- Have the child read the book independently.
- Invite them to list questions that arise from reading.

After Reading

- Discuss the child's questions. Talk about how they might find answers to those questions.
- Prompt the child to think more. Ask: How did the Declaration of Independence change the United States? If you could add anything to it, what would you add? Why?

Pogo Books are published by Jump!
3500 American Blvd W, Suite 150
Bloomington, MN 55431
www.jumplibrary.com

Copyright © 2026 Jump!
International copyright reserved in all countries.
No part of this book may be reproduced in any form without written permission from the publisher.

Jump! is a division of FlutterBee Education Group.

Library of Congress Cataloging-in-Publication Data

Names: Larsen, Josephine author
Title: Declaration of Independence / by Josephine Larsen.
Description: Bloomington, MN: Jump!, Inc., [2026]
Series: Writing that changed U.S. history | Includes index.
Audience: Ages 7-10
Identifiers: LCCN 2025028119 (print)
LCCN 2025028120 (ebook)
ISBN 9798896623465 hardcover
ISBN 9798896623472 paperback
ISBN 9798896623489 ebook
Subjects: LCSH: United States. Declaration of Independence–Signers | United States–Politics and government–1775-1783–Juvenile literature
Classification: LCC E221 .L38 2026 (print)
LCC E221 (ebook)
LC record available at https://lccn.loc.gov/2025028119
LC ebook record available at https://lccn.loc.gov/2025028120

Editor: Alyssa Sorenson
Designer: Emma Almgren-Bersie

Photo Credits: National Archives, cover (document), 10-11; mato181/Shutterstock, cover (flag); RODWORKS/Shutterstock, 1; SimoneN/Shutterstock, 3; Archive Photos/Getty, 4; PRISMA ARCHIVO/Alamy, 5; John Trumbull/Yale University Art Gallery/Wikimedia, 6-7; Library of Congress, 8; Niday Picture Library/Alamy, 9; Allan Ramsay/Indianapolis Museum of Art/Wikimedia, 12-13; f11photo/iStock, 14-15; Wikimedia, 16; John Trumbull/United States Capitol/Wikimedia, 16-17; Library Company of Philadelphia, 18; monkeybusinessimages/iStock, 19; Frame Stock Footage/Shutterstock, 20-21; dnaveh/iStock, 23.

Printed in the United States of America at Corporate Graphics in North Mankato, Minnesota.

TABLE OF CONTENTS

CHAPTER 1

THIRTEEN COLONIES

In the 1700s, Great Britain had **colonies** all around the world. Thirteen were on the East Coast of North America. Colonists lived there. The British government made laws for them.

Many colonists did not like the laws. Why? They did not have a say in them. They also had to pay **taxes** to Great Britain. Many colonists thought this was unfair. They spoke out.

The British government did not give them more **rights**. It sent soldiers to control the colonists. This started the Revolutionary War in 1775. It lasted eight years. During this time, the colonists fought for **independence**. They decided to create their own country.

TAKE A LOOK!

The 13 colonies became the first U.S. states. What were they? What areas did they cover in 1775? Take a look!

CHAPTER 2

THE DECLARATION

Colonists picked leaders. George Washington was one. These leaders formed the First Continental Congress in 1774. They met. They talked about the future of the colonies. A year later, they met again at the Second Continental Congress. This time, they made an army. Why? It would fight against Britain.

In 1776, they made a document. It was called the **Declaration** of Independence. It explained why the colonies should be free. It **encouraged** colonists to fight in the war. Thomas Jefferson wrote it.

IN CONGRESS, JULY 4, 1776.

The unanimous Declaration of the thirteen united States of America,

When in the Course of human events, it becomes necessary for one people to dissolve the political bands which have connected them with another, and to assume among the powers of the earth, the separate and equal station to which the Laws of Nature and of Nature's God entitle them, a decent respect to the opinions of mankind requires that they should declare the causes which impel them to the separation. —— We hold these truths to be self-evident, that all men are created equal, that they are endowed by their Creator with certain unalienable Rights, that among these are Life, Liberty and the pursuit of Happiness. — That to secure these rights, Governments are instituted among Men, deriving their just powers from the consent of the governed, — That whenever any Form of Government becomes destructive of these ends, it is the Right of the People to alter or to abolish it, and to institute new Government, laying its foundation on such principles and organizing its powers in such form, as to them shall seem most likely to effect their Safety and Happiness. Prudence, indeed, will dictate that Governments long established should not be changed for light and transient causes; and accordingly all experience hath shewn, that mankind are more disposed to suffer, while evils are sufferable, than to right themselves by abolishing the forms to which they are accustomed. But when a long train of abuses and usurpations, pursuing invariably the same Object evinces a design to reduce them under absolute Despotism, it is their right, it is their duty, to throw off such Government, and to provide new Guards for their future security. — Such has been the patient sufferance of these Colonies; and such is now the necessity which constrains them to alter their former Systems of Government. The history of the present King of Great Britain is a history of repeated injuries and usurpations, all having in direct object the establishment of an absolute Tyranny over these States. To prove this, let Facts be submitted to a candid world. —— He has refused his Assent to Laws, the most wholesome and necessary for the public good. —— He has forbidden his Governors to pass Laws of immediate and pressing importance, unless suspended in their operation till his Assent should be obtained; and when so suspended, he has utterly neglected to attend to them. —— He has refused to pass other Laws for the accommodation of large districts of people, unless those people would relinquish the right of Representation in the Legislature, a right inestimable to them and formidable to tyrants only. —— He has called together legislative bodies at places unusual, uncomfortable, and distant from the depository of their Public Records, for the sole purpose of fatiguing them into compliance with his measures. —— He has dissolved Representative Houses repeatedly, for opposing with manly firmness his invasions on the rights of the people. —— He has refused for a long time, after such dissolutions, to cause others to be elected; whereby the Legislative powers, incapable of Annihilation, have returned to the People at large for their exercise; the State remaining in the mean time exposed to all the dangers of invasion from without, and convulsions within. —— He has endeavoured to prevent the population of these States; for that purpose obstructing the Laws for Naturalization of Foreigners; refusing to pass others to encourage their migrations hither, and raising the conditions of new Appropriations of Lands. —— He has obstructed the Administration of Justice, by refusing his Assent to Laws for establishing Judiciary powers. —— He has made Judges dependent on his Will alone, for the tenure of their offices, and the amount and payment of their salaries. —— He has erected a multitude of New Offices, and sent hither swarms of Officers to harrass our people, and eat out their substance. —— He has kept among us, in times of peace, Standing Armies without the Consent of our legislatures. —— He has affected to render the Military independent of and superior to the Civil power. —— He has combined with others to subject us to a jurisdiction foreign to our constitution, and unacknowledged by our laws; giving his Assent to their Acts of pretended Legislation: — For Quartering large bodies of armed troops among us: — For protecting them, by a mock Trial, from punishment for any Murders which they should commit on the Inhabitants of these States: — For cutting off our Trade with all parts of the world: — For imposing Taxes on us without our Consent: — For depriving us in many cases, of the benefits of Trial by Jury: — For transporting us beyond Seas to be tried for pretended offences: — For abolishing the free System of English Laws in a neighbouring Province, establishing therein an Arbitrary government, and enlarging its Boundaries so as to render it at once an example and fit instrument for introducing the same absolute rule into these Colonies: — For taking away our Charters, abolishing our most valuable Laws, and altering fundamentally the Forms of our Governments: — For suspending our own Legislatures, and declaring themselves invested with power to legislate for us in all cases whatsoever. — He has abdicated Government here, by declaring us out of his Protection and waging War against us. —— He has plundered our seas, ravaged our Coasts, burnt our towns, and destroyed the lives of our people. —— He is at this time transporting large Armies of foreign Mercenaries to compleat the works of death, desolation and tyranny, already begun with circumstances of Cruelty & perfidy scarcely paralleled in the most barbarous ages, and totally unworthy the Head of a civilized nation. —— He has constrained our fellow Citizens taken Captive on the high Seas to bear Arms against their Country, to become the executioners of their friends and Brethren, or to fall themselves by their Hands. —— He has excited domestic insurrections amongst us, and has endeavoured to bring on the inhabitants of our frontiers, the merciless Indian Savages, whose known rule of warfare, is an undistinguished destruction of all ages, sexes and conditions. In every stage of these Oppressions We have Petitioned for Redress in the most humble terms: Our repeated Petitions have been answered only by repeated injury. A Prince, whose character is thus marked by every act which may define a Tyrant, is unfit to be the ruler of a free people. Nor have We been wanting in attentions to our Brittish brethren. We have warned them from time to time of attempts by their legislature to extend an unwarrantable jurisdiction over us. We have reminded them of the circumstances of our emigration and settlement here. We have appealed to their native justice and magnanimity, and we have conjured them by the ties of our common kindred to disavow these usurpations, which, would inevitably interrupt our connections and correspondence. They too have been deaf to the voice of justice and of consanguinity. We must, therefore, acquiesce in the necessity, which denounces our Separation, and hold them, as we hold the rest of mankind, Enemies in War, in Peace Friends. ——

We, therefore, the Representatives of the united States of America, in General Congress, Assembled, appealing to the Supreme Judge of the world for the rectitude of our intentions, do, in the Name, and by Authority of the good People of these Colonies, solemnly publish and declare, That these United Colonies are, and of Right ought to be Free and Independent States; that they are Absolved from all Allegiance to the British Crown, and that all political connection between them and the State of Great Britain, is and ought to be totally dissolved; and that as Free and Independent States, they have full Power to levy War, conclude Peace, contract Alliances, establish Commerce, and to do all other Acts and Things which Independent States may of right do. —— And for the support of this Declaration, with a firm reliance on the protection of divine Providence, we mutually pledge to each other our Lives, our Fortunes and our sacred Honor.

John Hancock

Button Gwinnett
Lyman Hall
Geo Walton.

Wm Hooper
Joseph Hewes,
John Penn

Edward Rutledge.
Thos Heyward Junr.
Thomas Lynch Junr.
Arthur Middleton

Samuel Chase
Wm Paca
Thos Stone
Charles Carroll of Carrollton

George Wythe
Richard Henry Lee
Th Jefferson
Benja Harrison
Thos Nelson jr.
Francis Lightfoot Lee
Carter Braxton

Robt Morris
Benjamin Rush
Benja. Franklin
John Morton
Geo Clymer
Jas. Smith
Geo. Taylor
James Wilson
Geo. Ross

Caesar Rodney
Geo Read
Thos M:Kean

Wm Floyd
Phil. Livingston
Frans. Lewis
Lewis Morris

Richd. Stockton
Jno Witherspoon
Fras. Hopkinson
John Hart
Abra Clark

Josiah Bartlett
Wm Whipple
Saml Adams
John Adams
Robt Treat Paine
Elbridge Gerry
Step. Hopkins
William Ellery
Roger Sherman
Sam el Huntington
Wm Williams
Oliver Wolcott
Matthew Thornton

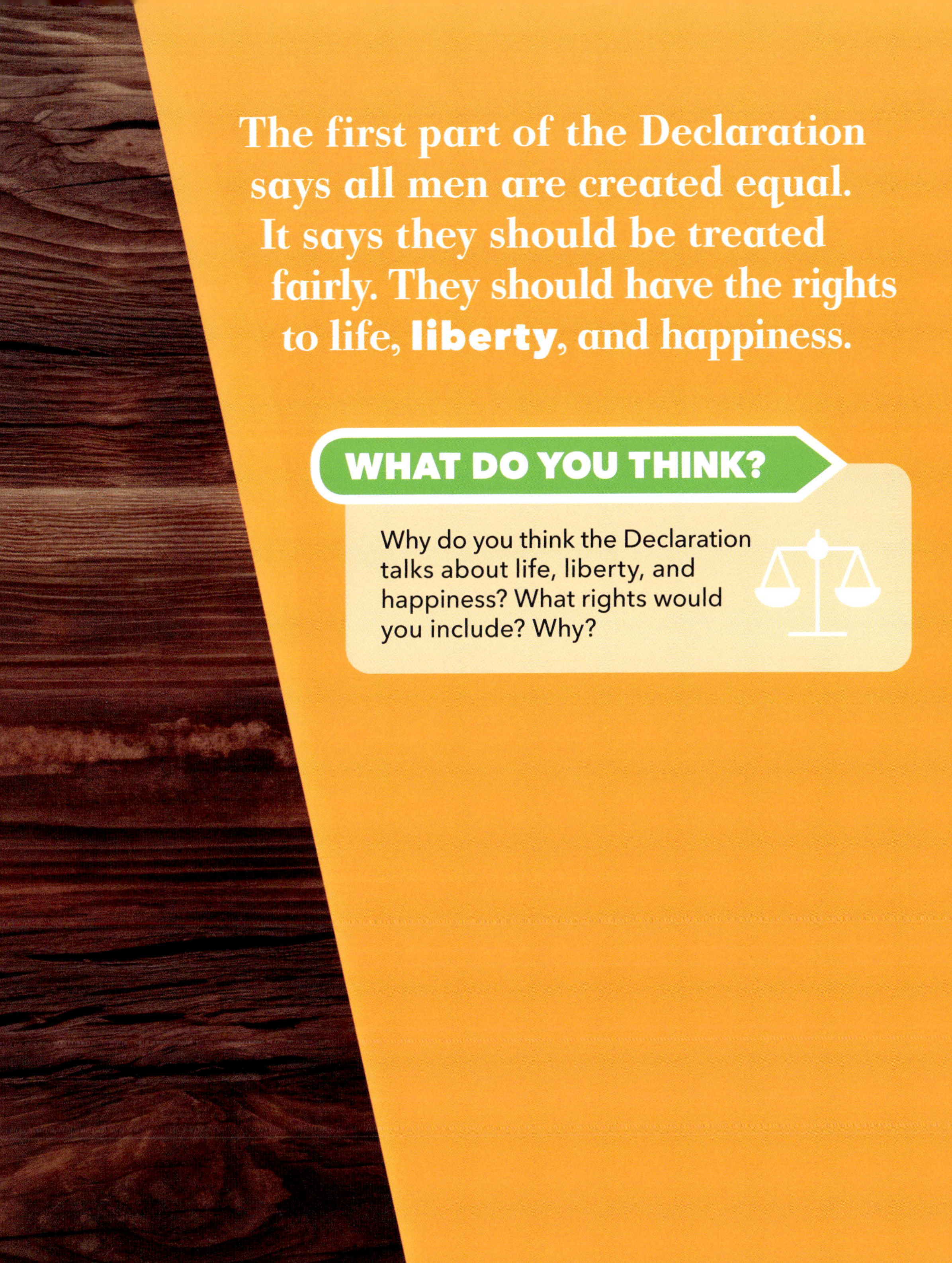

The first part of the Declaration says all men are created equal. It says they should be treated fairly. They should have the rights to life, **liberty**, and happiness.

WHAT DO YOU THINK?

Why do you think the Declaration talks about life, liberty, and happiness? What rights would you include? Why?

The second part is about Britain's King George III. It has **complaints** against him. It explains why colonists did not want to be ruled by him. Why? One reason was he did not give them fair **trials**.

DID YOU KNOW?

There are 27 complaints about King George III in the document.

King George III

Independence Hall

The document ends by saying the colonies would not follow British laws. They were now a free country. It would later be called the United States of America.

Congress had to vote on independence. Leaders met in the Pennsylvania State House. It is now called Independence Hall. It is in Philadelphia. On July 2, 1776, the vote passed.

Two days later, Congress **approved** the Declaration. The date was July 4, 1776. A final copy was written on **parchment**. Leaders signed it on August 2.

The Declaration was printed in newspapers. People liked what it said. It gave them hope for a better future.

(335)

The PENNSYLVANIA EVENING POST.

Price only Two Coppers. Publiſhed every *Tueſday*, *Thurſday*, and *Saturday* Evenings.

Vol. II.] SATURDAY, JULY 6, 1776. [Num. 228.

In CONGRESS, July 4, 1776.
A Declaration by the Repreſentatives of the United States of America, in General Congreſs aſſembled.

WHEN, in the courſe of human events, it becomes neceſſary for one people to diſſolve the political bands which have connected them with another, and to aſſume, among the powers of the earth, the ſeparate and equal ſtation to which the laws of nature and of nature's God intitle them, a decent reſpect to the opinions of mankind requires that they ſhould declare the cauſes which impel them to the ſeparation.

We hold theſe truths to be ſelf-evident, That all men are created equal; that they are endowed, by their Creator, with certain unalienable rights; that among theſe are life, liberty, and the purſuit of happineſs. That to ſecure theſe rights, governments are inſtituted among men, deriving their juſt powers from the conſent of the governed; that whenever any form of government becomes deſtructive of theſe ends, it is the right of the people to alter or to aboliſh it, and to inſtitute new government, laying its foundation on ſuch principles, and organizing its powers in ſuch form, as to them ſhall ſeem moſt likely to effect their ſafety and happineſs. Prudence, indeed, will dictate that governments long eſtabliſhed ſhould not be changed for light and tranſient cauſes; and accordingly all experience hath ſhewn, that mankind are more diſpoſed to ſuffer, while evils are ſufferable, than to right themſelves by aboliſhing the forms to which they are accuſtomed. But when a long train of abuſes and uſurpations, purſuing invariably the ſame object, evinces a deſign to reduce them under abſolute deſpotiſm, it is their right, it is their duty, to throw off ſuch government, and to provide new guards for their future ſecurity. Such has been the patient ſufferance of theſe colonies, and ſuch is now the neceſſity which conſtrains them to alter their former ſyſtems of government. The hiſtory of the preſent King of Great-Britain is a hiſtory of repeated injuries and uſurpations, all having in direct object the eſtabliſhment of an abſolute tyranny over theſe ſtates. To prove this, let facts be ſubmitted to a candid world.

He has refuſed his aſſent to laws, the moſt wholeſome and neceſſary for the public good.

He has forbidden his Governors to paſs laws of immediate and preſſing importance, unleſs ſuſpended in their operation till his aſſent ſhould be obtained; and, when ſo ſuſpended, he has utterly neglected to attend to them.

He has refuſed to paſs other laws for the accommodation of large diſtricts of people, unleſs thoſe people would relinquiſh the right of repreſentation in the legiſlature, a right ineſtimable to them, and formidable to tyrants only.

He has called together legiſlative bodies at places unuſual, uncomfortable, and diſtant from the depoſitory of their public records, for the ſole purpoſe of fatiguing them into compliance with his meaſures.

He has diſſolved Repreſentative Houſes repeatedly, for oppoſing with manly firmneſs his invaſions on the rights of the people.

He has refuſed for a long time, after ſuch diſſolutions, to cauſe others to be elected; whereby the legiſlative powers, incapable of annihilation, have returned to the people at large for their exerciſe; the ſtate remaining in the mean time expoſed to all the dangers of invaſion from without, and convulſions within.

He has endeavoured to prevent the population of theſe ſtates; for that purpoſe obſtructing the laws for naturalization of foreigners; refuſing to paſs others to encourage their migrations hither, and raiſing the conditions of new appropriations of lands.

He has obſtructed the adminiſtration of juſtice, by refuſing his aſſent to laws for eſtabliſhing judiciary powers.

He has made Judges dependant on his will alone, for the tenure of their offices, and the amount and payment of their ſalaries.

He has erected a multitude of new offices, and ſent hither ſwarms of officers to harraſs our people, and eat out their ſubſtance.

He has kept among us, in times of peace, ſtanding armies, without the conſent of our legiſlatures.

He has affected to render the military independant of and ſuperior to the civil power.

He has combined with others to ſubject us to a juriſdiction foreign to our conſtitution, and unacknowledged by our laws; giving his aſſent to their acts of pretended legiſlation:

For quartering large bodies of armed troops among us:

For protecting them, by a mock trial, from puniſhment for any murders which they ſhould commit on the inhabitants of theſe ſtates:

For cutting off our trade with all parts of the world:

For impoſing taxes on us without our conſent:

For depriving us, in many caſes, of the benefits of trial by jury:

For tranſporting us beyond ſeas to be tried for pretended offences:

For aboliſhing the free ſyſtem of Engliſh laws in a neighbouring province, eſtabliſhing therein an arbitrary government, and enlarging its boundaries, ſo as to render it at once an example and fit inſtrument for introducing the ſame abſolute rule into theſe colonies:

For taking away our charters, aboliſhing our moſt valuable laws, and altering fundamentally the forms of our governments:

For ſuſpending our own legiſlatures, and declaring themſelves inveſted with power to legiſlate for us in all caſes whatſoever.

He has abdicated government here, by declaring us out of his protection and waging war againſt us.

He has plundered our ſeas, ravaged our coaſts, burnt our towns, and deſtroyed the lives of our people.

He is, at this time, tranſporting large armies of foreign mercenaries to complete the works of death, deſolation, and tyranny, already begun with circumſtances of cruelty and

CHAPTER 3

FOREVER FREE

The Declaration encouraged people to fight for their freedom. The United States won the war in 1783. It was free from British rule!

Independence Day is a holiday in the United States. It is also called the Fourth of July. It celebrates the **anniversary** of the Declaration passing.

HOW TO MARK
YOUR PAPER BALLOT

The Declaration of Independence was written more than 200 years ago. How does it affect your life today? What would life be like if it had never been created?

WHAT DO YOU THINK?

The Declaration told the world the United States was free. Do you think having freedom is important? Why or why not?

QUICK FACTS & TOOLS

TIMELINE

What are important dates in the history of the Declaration of Independence? Take a look!

SEPTEMBER 5, 1774
Leaders meet for the First Continental Congress. They talk about the future of the colonies.

APRIL 19, 1775
The Revolutionary War starts with the Battles of Lexington and Concord.

MAY 10, 1775
Leaders meet at the Second Continental Congress.

JUNE 11, 1776
Thomas Jefferson starts writing the Declaration of Independence.

JULY 4, 1776
The Second Continental Congress approves the Declaration.

AUGUST 2, 1776
Most members of the Second Continental Congress sign the Declaration. This includes John Hancock, Benjamin Franklin, and Thomas Jefferson.

SEPTEMBER 3, 1783
The United States wins the Revolutionary War. It gains freedom from Great Britain.

GLOSSARY

anniversary: A date that people remember each year because of an important event that happened on that date in an earlier year.

approved: Officially accepted.

colonies: Areas that have been settled by people from another country and are controlled by that country.

complaints: Statements that show unhappiness about something.

declaration: An announcement.

encouraged: Gave someone the confidence to do something.

independence: Freedom.

liberty: The state of being free.

parchment: Material made from animal skins that is used to write on.

rights: Things you are allowed to do.

taxes: Money that people and businesses must pay in order to support a government.

trials: Examinations of evidence in a court of law to decide if someone is guilty or innocent.

INDEX

TO LEARN MORE

Finding more information is as easy as 1, 2, 3.

1. Go to www.factsurfer.com
2. Enter "Declaration of Independence" into the search box.
3. Choose your book to see a list of websites.